FINGERPICKING LOVE songs

T0081542

INTRODUCTION TO FINGERSTYLE GUITAR

Fingerstyle (a.k.a. fingerpicking) is a guitar technique that means you literally pick the strings with your right-hand fingers and thumb. This contrasts with the conventional technique of strumming and playing single notes with a pick (a.k.a. flatpicking). For fingerpicking, you can use any type of guitar: acoustic steel-string, nylon-string classical, or electric.

THE RIGHT HAND

The most common right-hand position is shown here.

Use a high wrist; arch your palm as if you were holding a ping-pong ball. Keep the thumb outside and away from the fingers, and let the fingers do the work rather than lifting your whole hand.

The thumb generally plucks the bottom strings with downstrokes on the left side of the thumb and thumbnail. The other fingers pluck the higher strings using upstrokes with the fleshy tip of the fingers and fingernails. The thumb and fingers should pluck one string per stroke and not brush over several strings.

Another picking option you may choose to use is called hybrid picking (a.k.a. plectrum-style fingerpicking). Here, the pick is usually held between the thumb and first finger, and the three remaining fingers are assigned to pluck the higher strings.

THE LEFT HAND

The left-hand fingers are numbered 1 through 4.

Be sure to keep your fingers arched, with each joint bent; if they flatten out across the strings, they will deaden the sound when you fingerpick. As a general rule, let the strings ring as long as possible when playing fingerstyle.

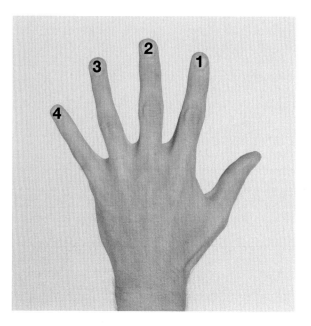

Back at One

Words and Music by Brian McKnight

Drop D tuning:
(low to high) D-A-D-G-B-E

Verse
Slowly

1. It's un- de- ni- a- ble that we should be __ to- geth- er.
2. It's so in- cred- i- ble, the way things work __ them- selves out.

It's un- be- liev- a- ble how I used to say __ that I'd fall nev- er.
And all e- mo- tion- al, once you know what __ it's all __ a- bout, __ hey.

The ba- sis is need __ to know. If you don't know just how __ I feel, __ then
And un- de- sir- a- ble, for us to be __ a- part. __

let me show ___ you now ___ that I'm ___ for real. ___
Nev - er would ___ have made ___ it ver - y far, ___

If
'cause you

all things ___ in time, ___ time will ___ re - veal. ___
know you've got the keys _____ to ___ my heart. ___

Yeah, _____

𝄋 Chorus

(1., 2.) one, ⎫
    3. One, ⎭

you're like a dream come true. Two, just wan - na be with you.

Three,   girl, it's plain to see   that you're the on - ly one __ for me. __ And

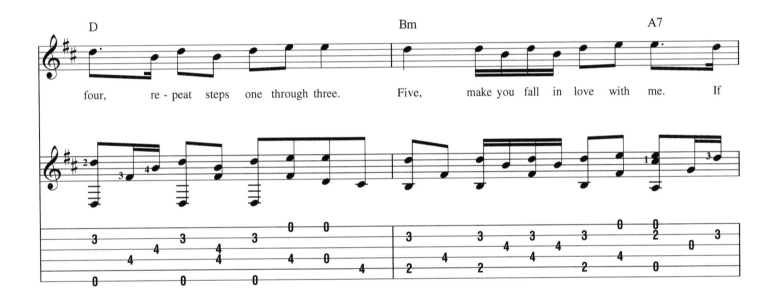

four, re - peat steps one through three.   Five,   make you fall in love with me.   If

1.

To Coda ⊕

ev - er I __ be - lieve __ my work __ is done, __   then I'll start __ back __ at one. __

came and breathed __ new __ life __ in - to __ this   lone - ly heart __ of mine. _____   You

D.S. al Coda

threw   out ___ the life - line,   just   in   the   nick ___ of   time. _____

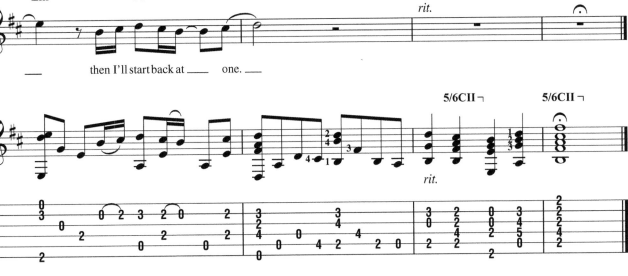

⊕ **Coda**

then I'll start back at ___ one. ___

Glory of Love

Theme from KARATE KID PART II
Words and Music by David Foster, Peter Cetera and Diane Nini

lone.

Verse

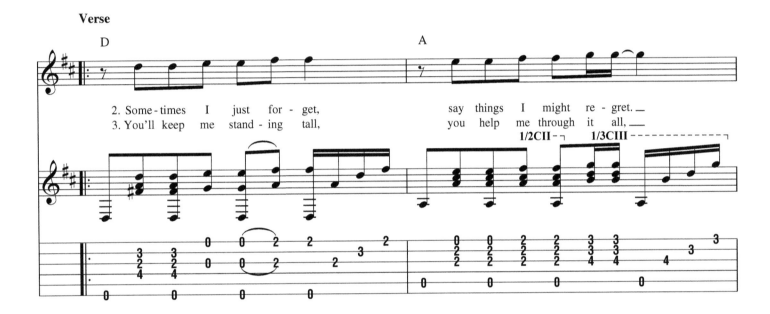

2. Some - times I just for - get, say things I might re - gret. ___
3. You'll keep me stand - ing tall, you help me through it all, ___

It breaks my heart to see ___ you cry - ing.
I'm al - ways strong when you're ___ be - side me.

I don't want to lose you,_____
I have al - ways need - ed ___ you.

I could nev - er make it ___ a -
I could nev - er make it ___ a -

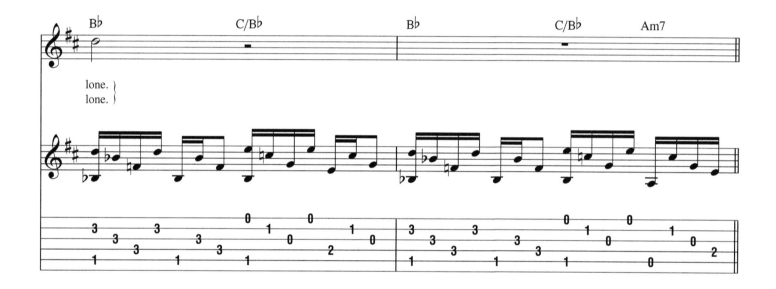

lone.
lone.

% Chorus

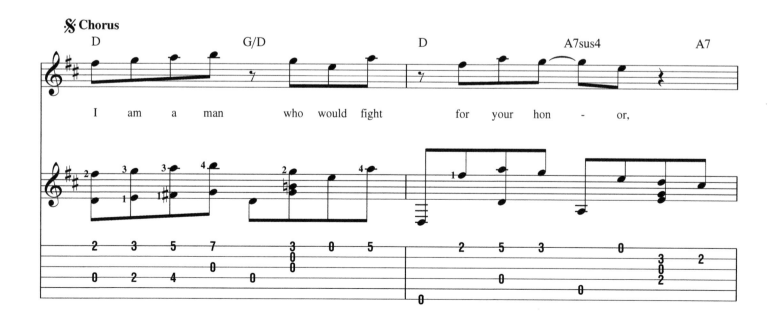

I am a man   who would fight   for your hon - or,

I'll be the he - ro you're ____ dream - ing of. ____

We'll live for - ev - er, know - ing to - geth - er that we

To Coda ⊕

did it all for the glo - ry of

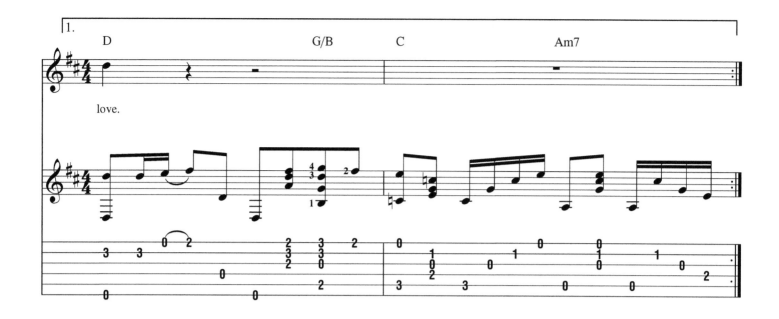

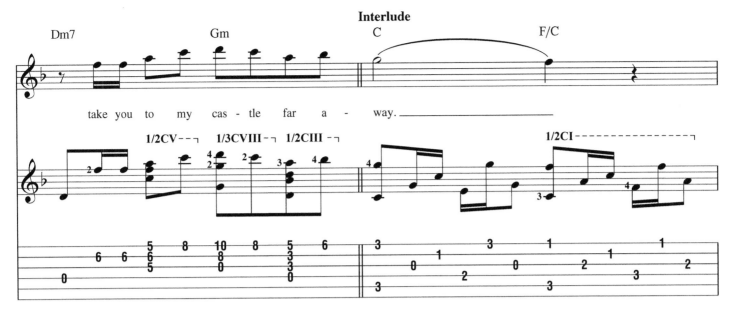

take you to my cas - tle far a - way. _____

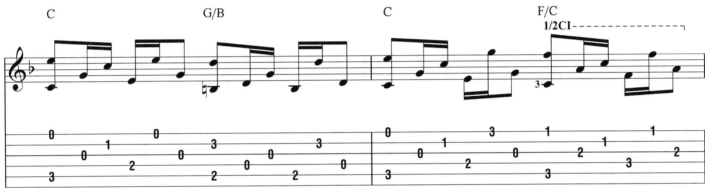

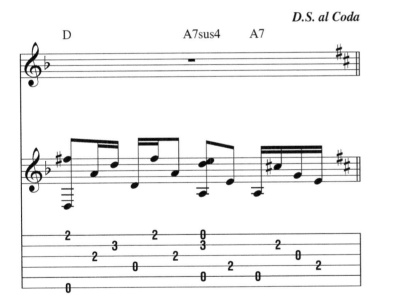

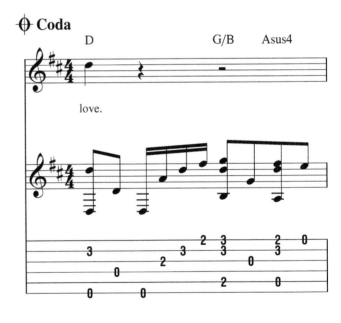

A Groovy Kind of Love

Words and Music by Toni Wine and Carole Bayer Sager

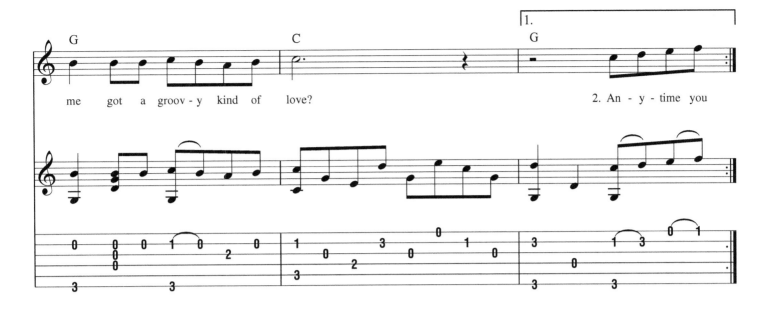

me got a groov-y kind of love? 2. An - y - time you

3. When I'm feel - in' blue, all I have to do is take a look at

you, then I'm not so blue. When I'm in your arms, noth - ing seems to

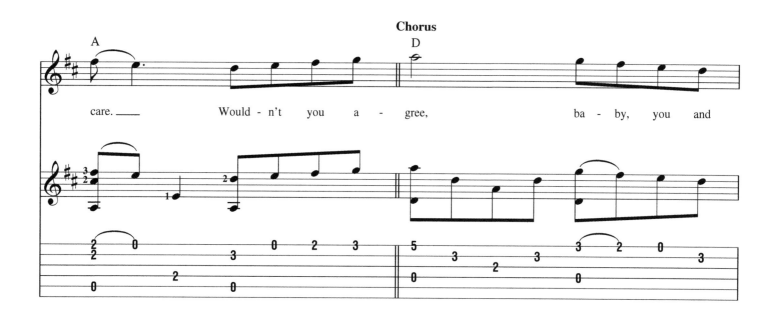

Chorus

Outro

We got a groov-y kind of love.

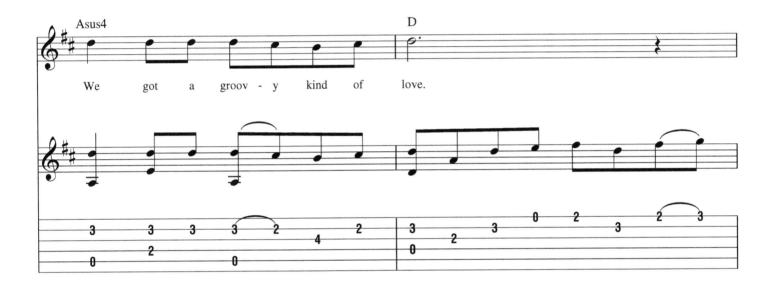

We got a groov-y kind of love.

Whoa, _____ We got a groov-y kind of love.

I Believe in You and Me

from the Touchstone Motion Picture THE PREACHER'S WIFE
Words and Music by David Wolfert and Sandy Linzer

love will nev - er end. ____   And like the riv - er finds ____ the sea, I ____   was

lost, ____   now I'm free   'cause   I   be - lieve ___ in you and

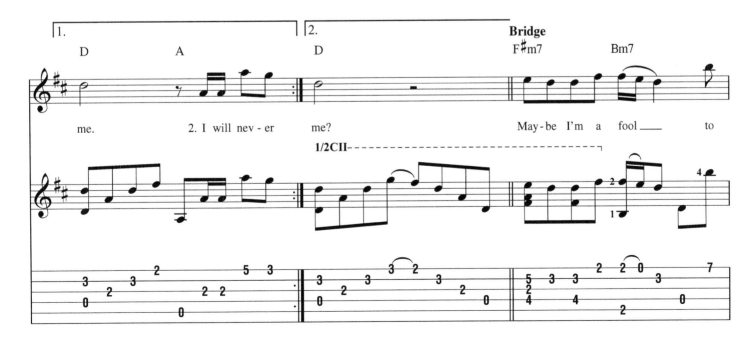

me.   2. I will nev - er   me?   May - be I'm a fool ____   to

feel the way __ I do.   I would play the fool for-ev-er   just to be with you for-ev-er. _____

Verse

_____ 3. I be-lieve in   mir-a-cles, _____   and love's _____ a mir-a-cle. ___   And yes,

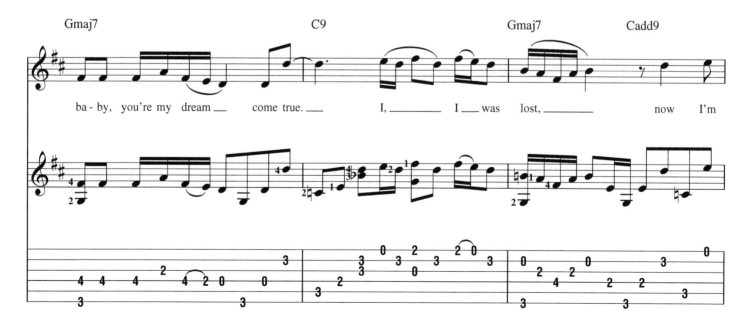

ba-by, you're my dream __ come true. ___   I, _____ I __ was   lost, _____   now I'm

free, _____ oh, ba - by, 'cause I be - lieve, _ I do be - lieve in you and me. See, I'm ___

Outro

lost _____ now I'm free _____ 'cause

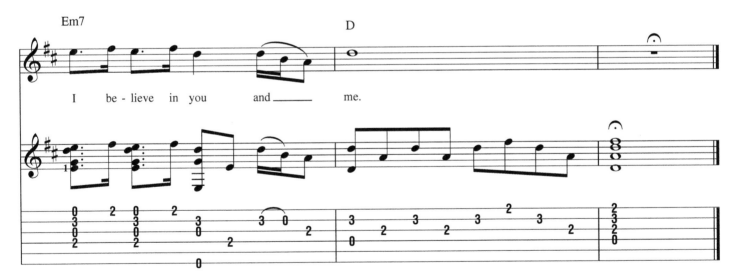

I be - lieve in you and _____ me.

Additional Lyrics

2. I will never leave your side.
I will never hurt your pride.
When all the chips are down, babe,
Then I will always be around,
Just to be right where you are, my love.
You know I love you, boy.
I'll never leave you out.
I will always let you in, boy,
Oh, baby, to places no one's ever been.
Deep inside, can't you see
That I believe in you and me?

I Will

Words and Music by John Lennon and Paul McCartney

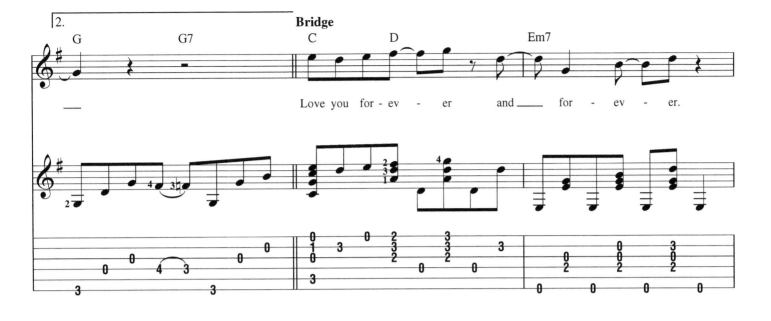

Love you for - ev - er and ____ for - ev - er.

Love you with all ____ my heart. ____ Love you when - ev - er we're ____

____ to - geth - er. Love you when we're ____ a - part. 3. And when ____

Verse

at last I find you, this song will fill the air.

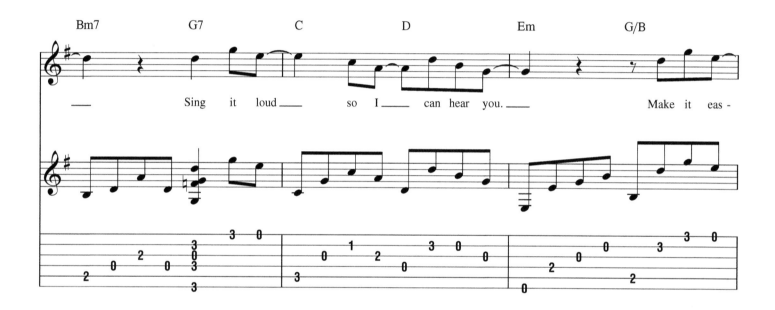

Sing it loud so I can hear you. Make it eas -

- y to be near you. For the things you do en - dear

How Deep Is Your Love

from the Motion Picture SATURDAY NIGHT FEVER
Words and Music by Barry Gibb, Robin Gibb and Maurice Gibb

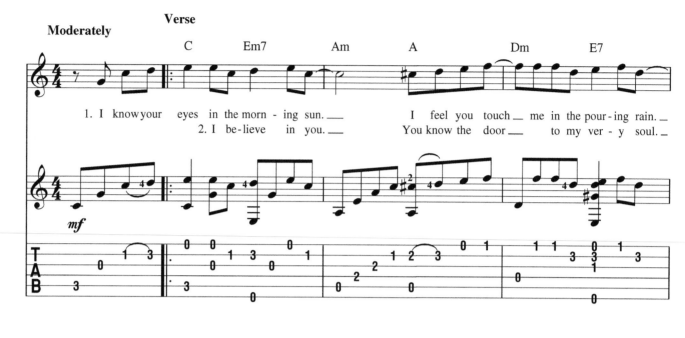

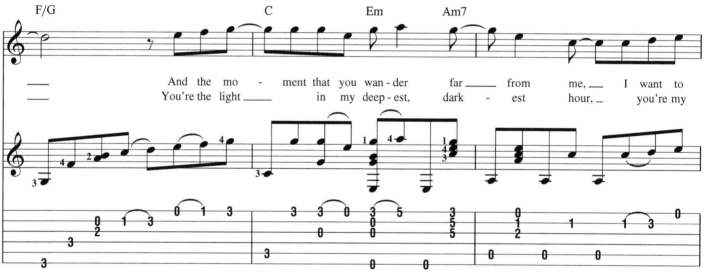

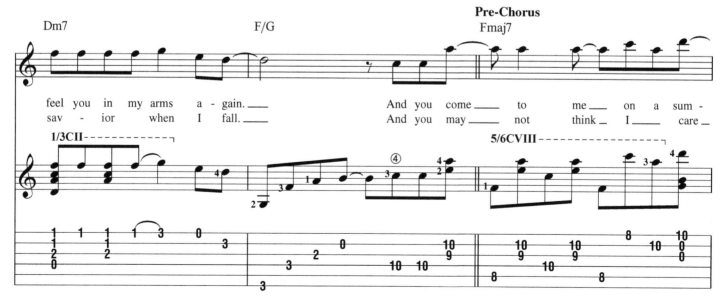

break-ing us down   when they all ___ should let us   be.   We be-long ___

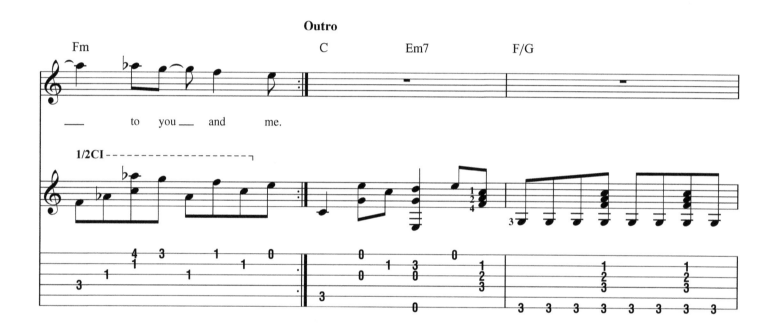

Outro

to   you ___ and   me.

How deep ___ is your love? ___ How   deep ___ is   your ___ love?

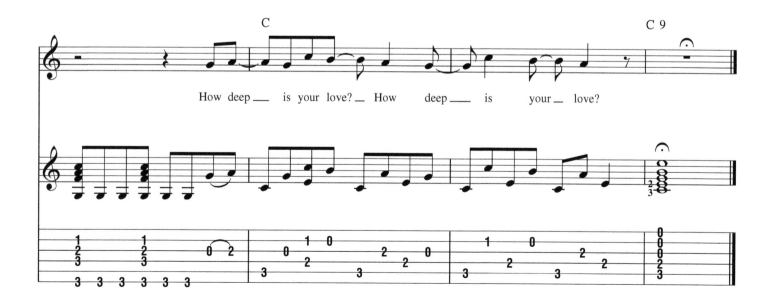

Maybe I'm Amazed

Words and Music by Paul McCartney

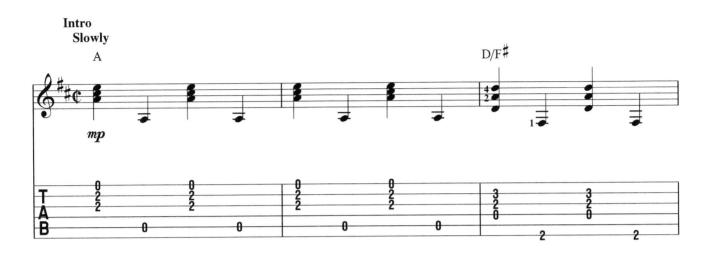

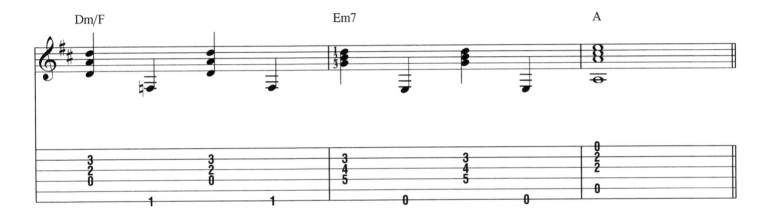

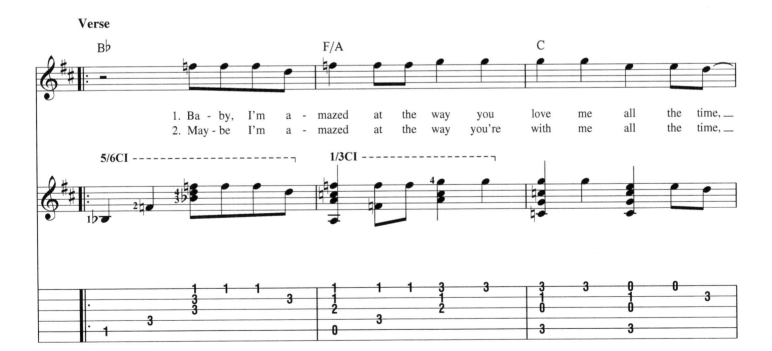

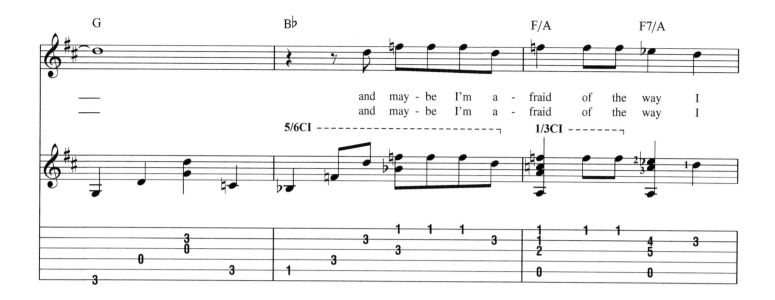

and may-be I'm a - fraid of the way I
and may-be I'm a - fraid of the way I

love you.
need you.

May-be I'm a -
Ba - by, I'm a -

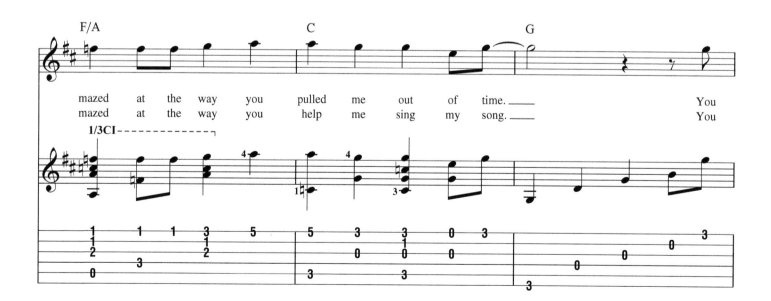

mazed at the way you pulled me out of time. ___
mazed at the way you help me sing my song. ___

You
You

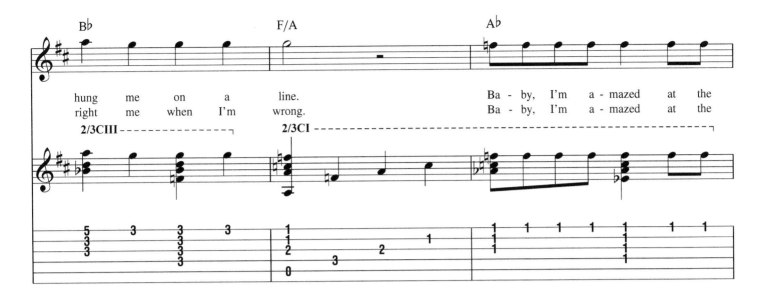

hung   me   on   a   line.   Ba - by,   I'm   a - mazed   at   the

right   me   when   I'm   wrong.   Ba - by,   I'm   a - mazed   at   the

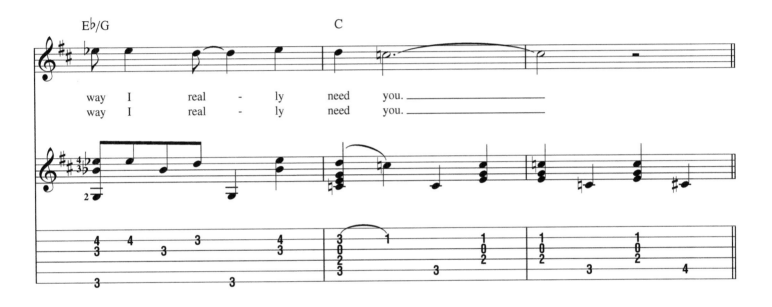

way   I   real - ly   need   you. _____

way   I   real - ly   need   you. _____

Chorus

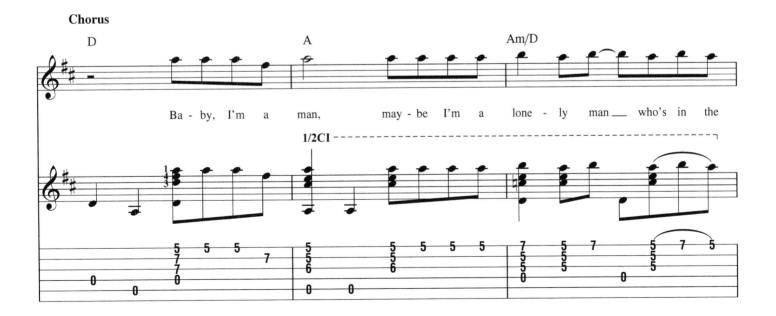

Ba - by,   I'm   a   man,   may - be   I'm   a   lone - ly   man ___ who's   in   the

mid - dle of some - thing ___ that he does - n't real - ly un - der - stand. ___

Ba - by, I'm a

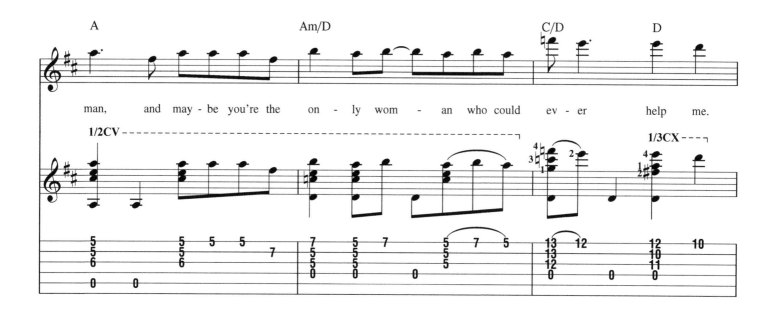

man, and may - be you're the on - ly wom - an who could ev - er help me.

Ba - by, won't you help me to ___ un - der - stand? ___ Ooh, ___

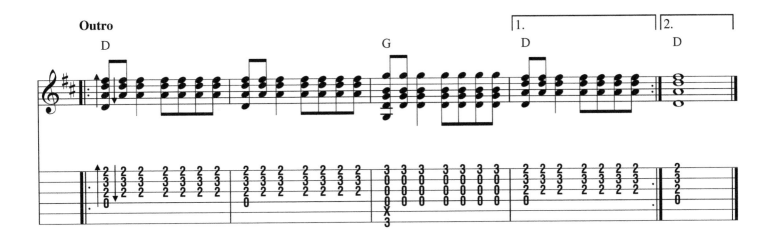

On the Wings of Love

Words and Music by Jeffrey Osborne and Peter Schless

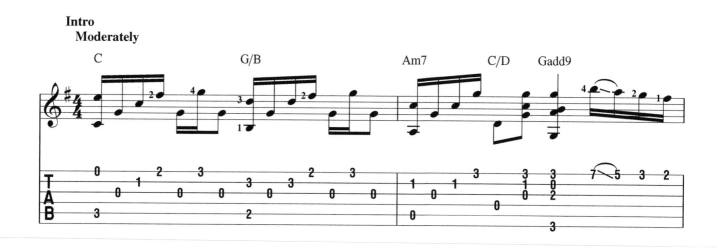

To Coda 1 ⊕

On the wings _ of love, _ up and a - bove the clouds; _ the on - ly way _ to fly _

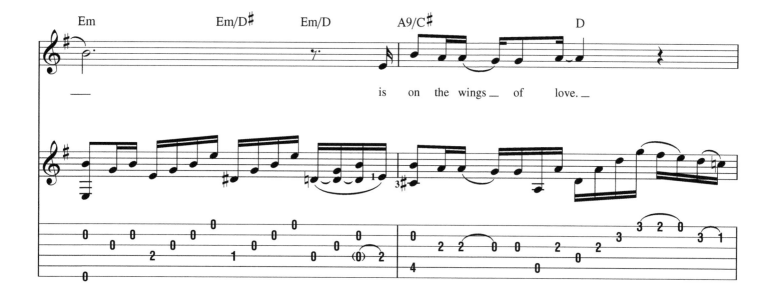

_ is on the wings _ of love. _

On the wings _ of love, _ on - ly the two of us _ to - geth - er fly - ing high;

To Coda 2

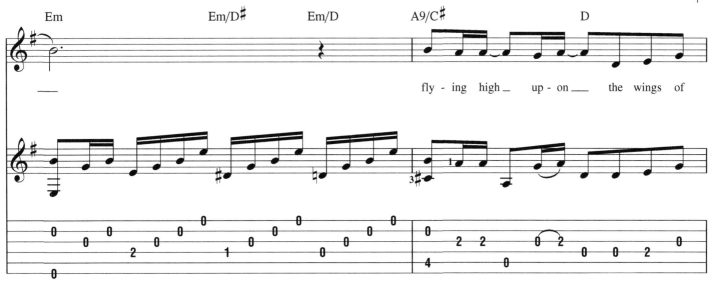

fly - ing high __ up - on __ the wings of

Coda 1

D.S. al Coda 1

love. ____

D.S.S. al Coda 2

you would come _ with me. __

Coda 2

Bridge

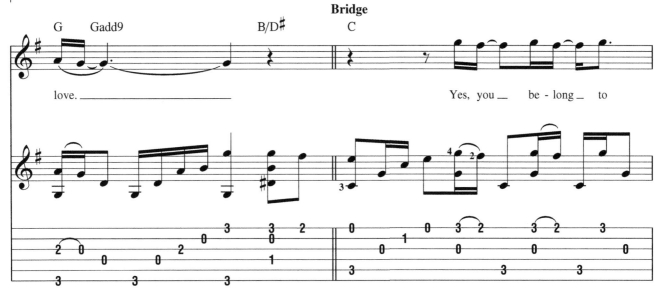

love. ____

Yes, you __ be - long __ to

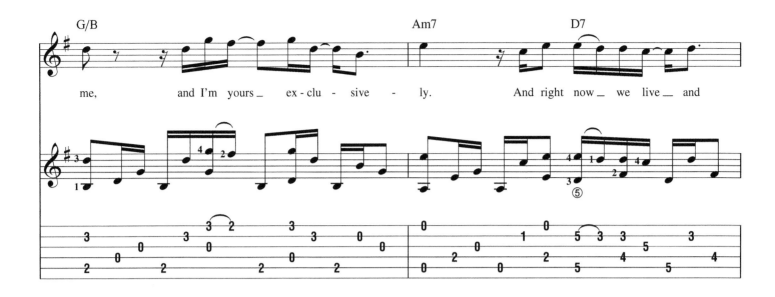

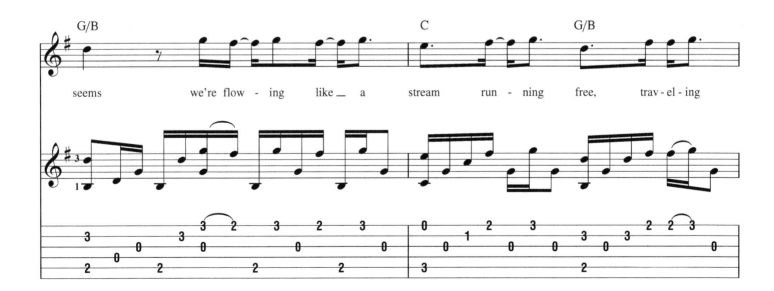

Outro-Chorus

on the wings _ of love. _   On the wings _ of love, _ up and a-

bove the clouds; _ the on - ly way _ to fly _   is

on the wings _ of love. _   On the wings of love, _ on - ly the

two of us ___ to-geth - er fly - ing high, ___ to - geth-er fly - ing high. ___

fly - ing high ___ up-on ___ the wings of love, _____

of love. _____

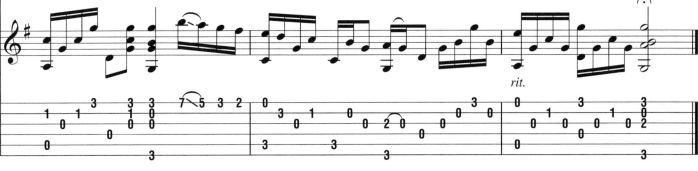

Put Your Head on My Shoulder

Words and Music by Paul Anka

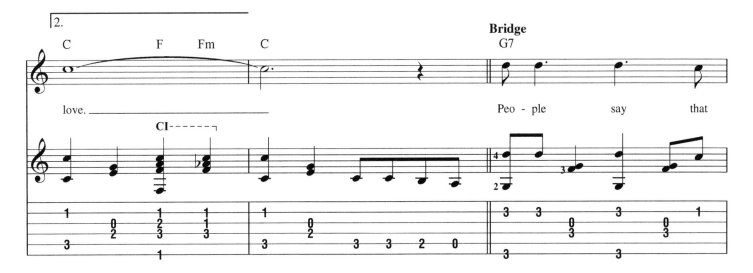

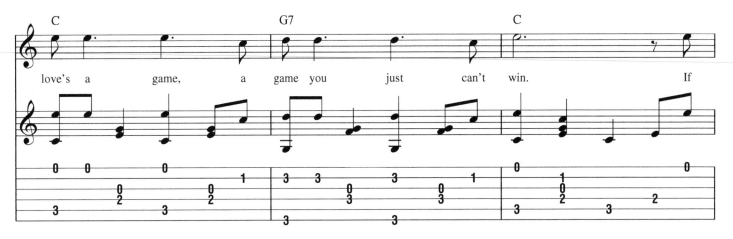

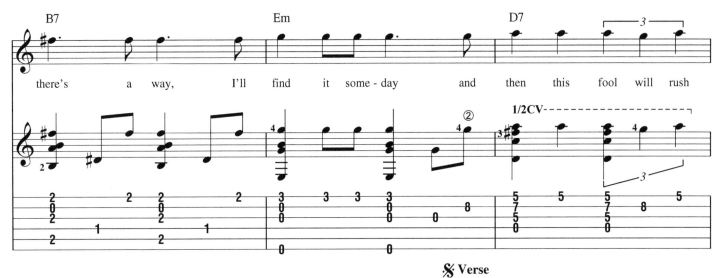

whis-per in my ear, ba - by, words I want to hear. Tell me,

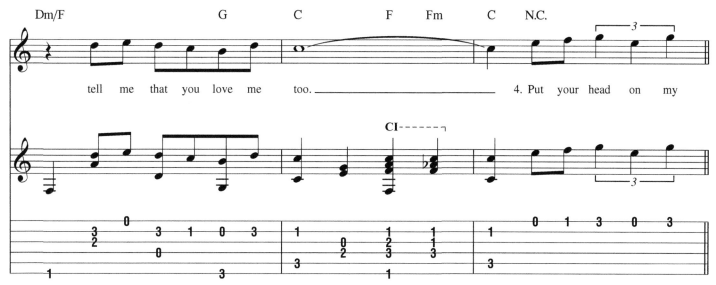

tell me that you love me too. _____ 4. Put your head on my

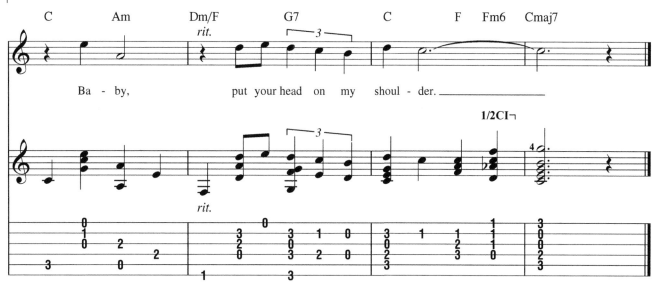

Ba - by, put your head on my shoul - der. _____

Somewhere Out There

from AN AMERICAN TAIL
Music by Barry Mann and James Horner
Lyric by Cynthia Weil

Verse
Slowly

1. Some - where out there be - neath the pale moon-

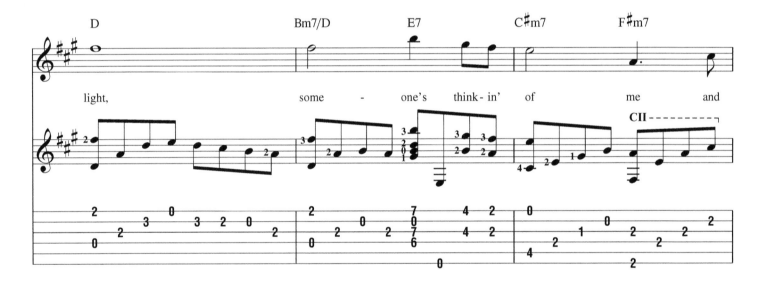

light, some - one's think - in' of me and

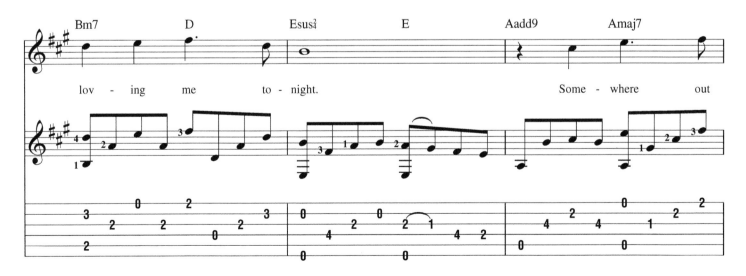

lov - ing me to - night. Some - where out

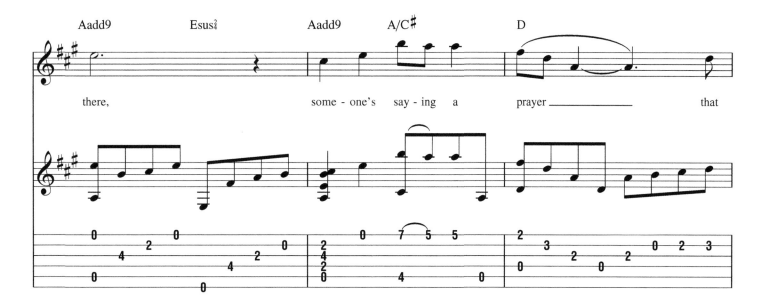

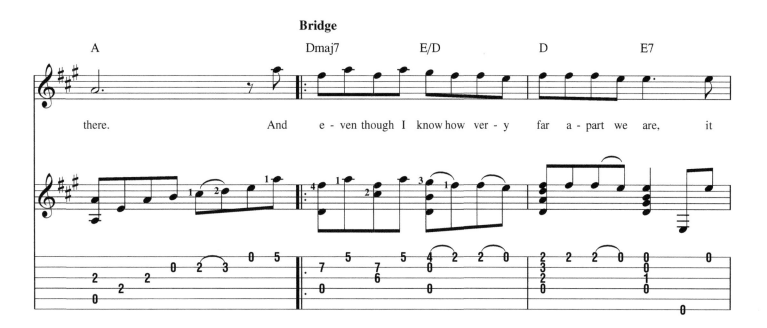

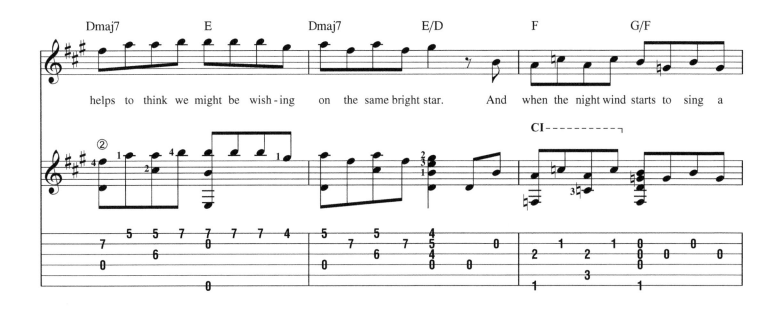

helps to think we might be wish - ing   on the same bright star.   And   when the night wind starts to sing a

lone - some lul - la - by,   it   helps to think we're sleep - ing un - der - - neath the same big

Verse

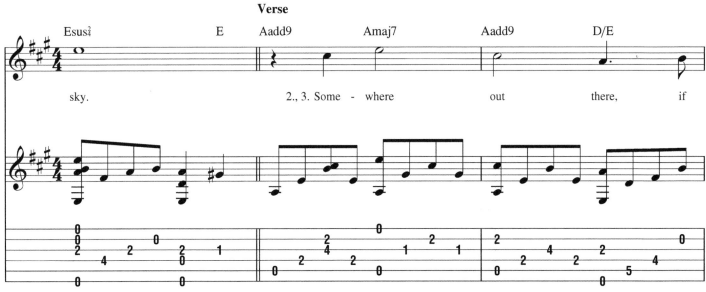

sky.   2., 3. Some - where   out   there,   if

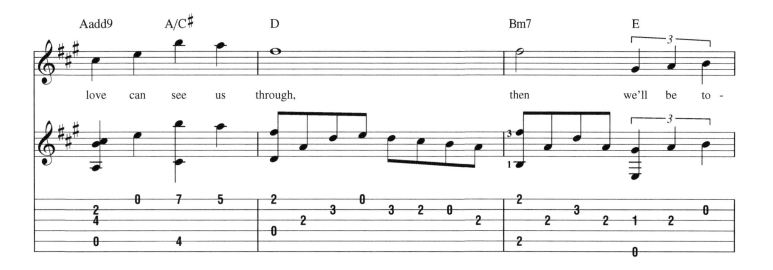

love can see us through, then we'll be to -

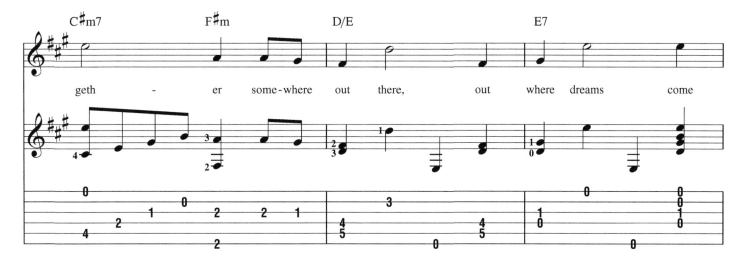

geth - er some-where out there, out where dreams come

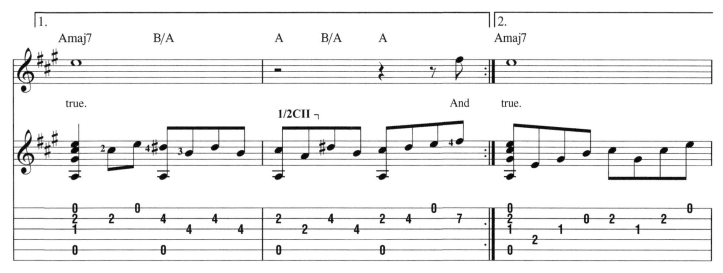

true. And true.

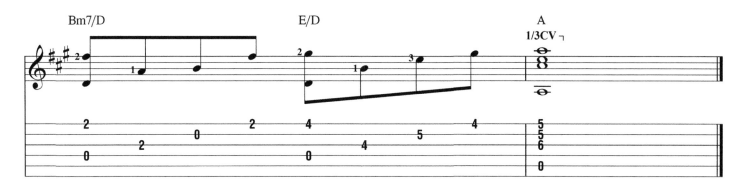

Three Times a Lady

Words and Music by Lionel Richie

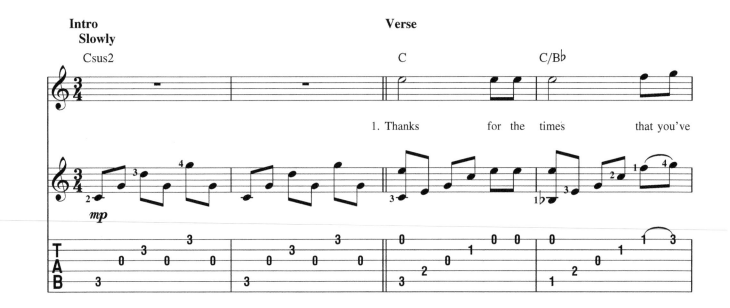

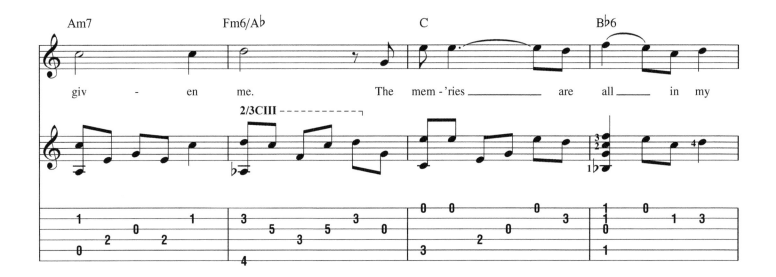

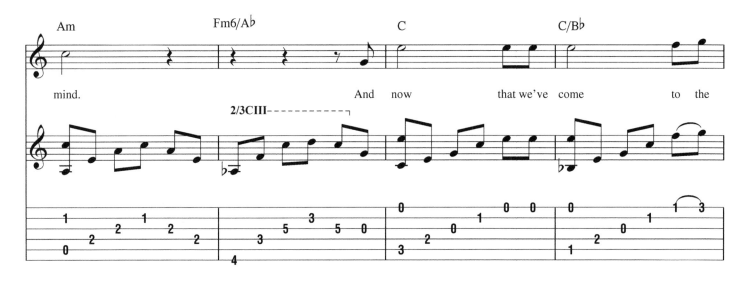

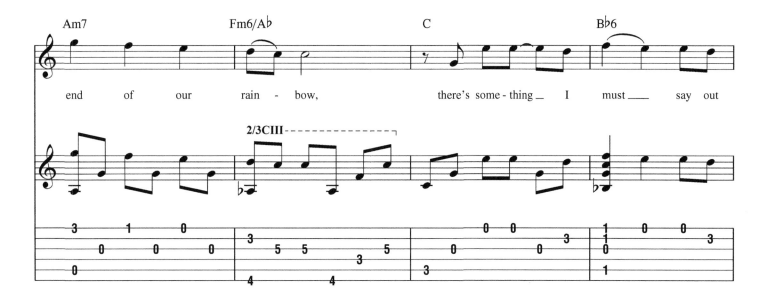

end   of   our   rain - bow,   there's some - thing __ I   must ___ say   out

loud: You're   once,

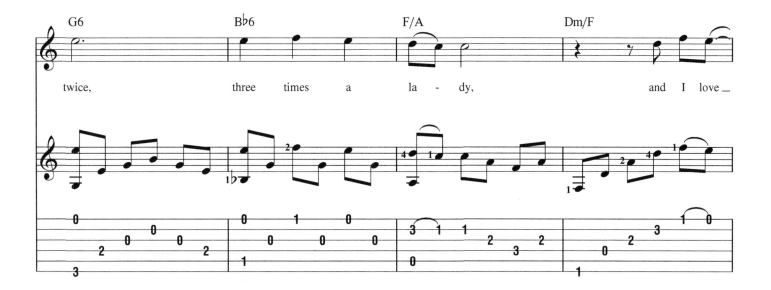

twice,   three   times   a   la - dy,   and   I   love __

you.   Yes, you're   once,

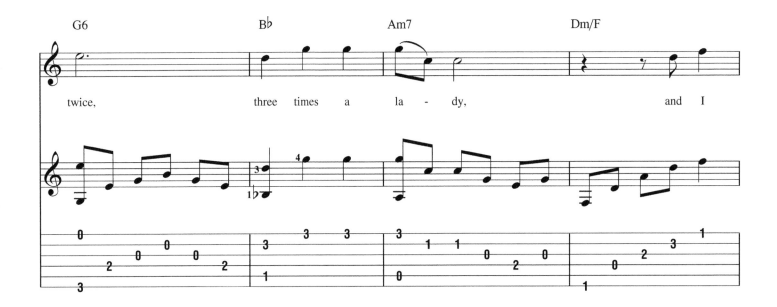

twice,   three times   a   la - dy,   and   I

Interlude

love _____ you.   I

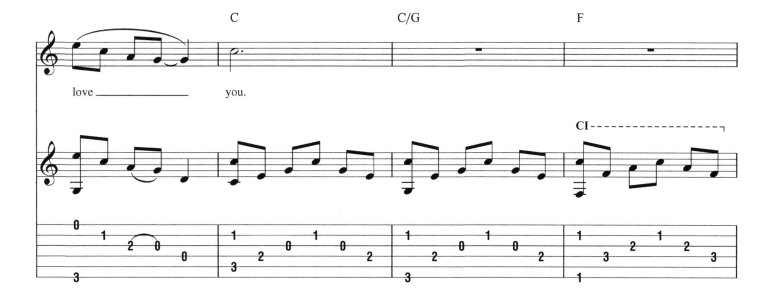

love _____ you.

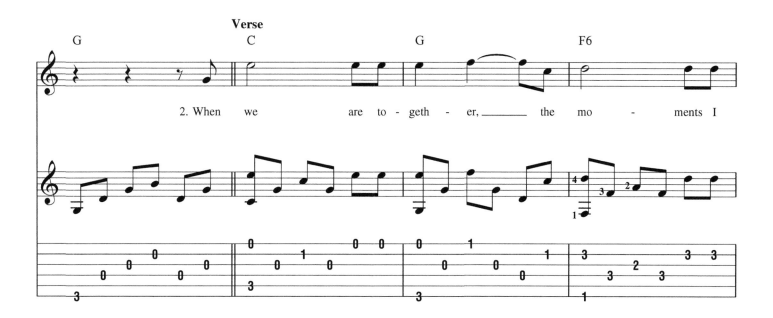

2. When we are to - geth - er, _____ the mo - ments I

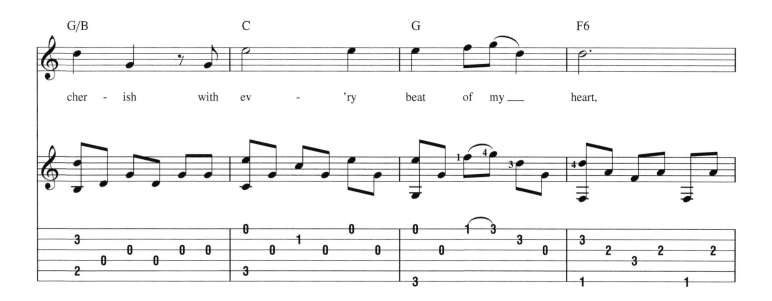

cher - ish with ev - 'ry beat of my ___ heart,

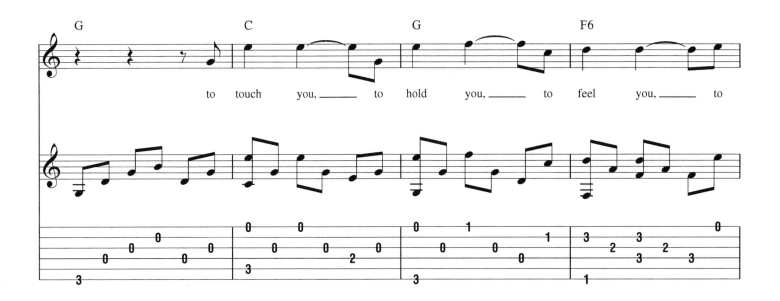

to touch you, _____ to hold you, _____ to feel you, _____ to

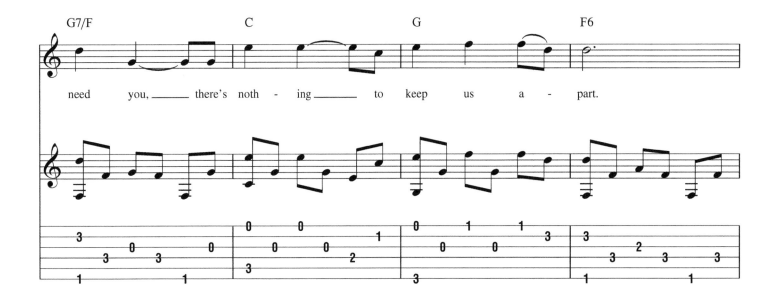

need you, _____ there's noth - ing _____ to keep us a - part.

Outro-Chorus

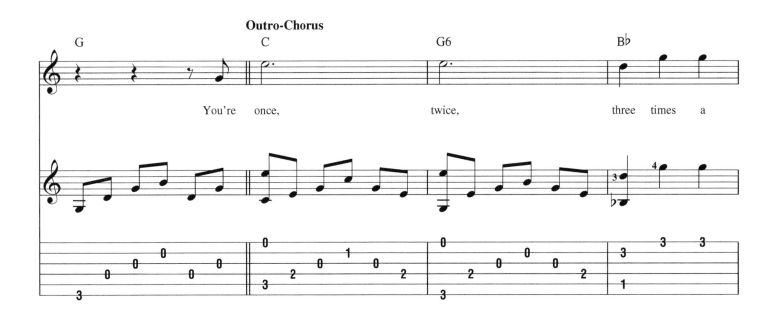

You're once, twice, three times a

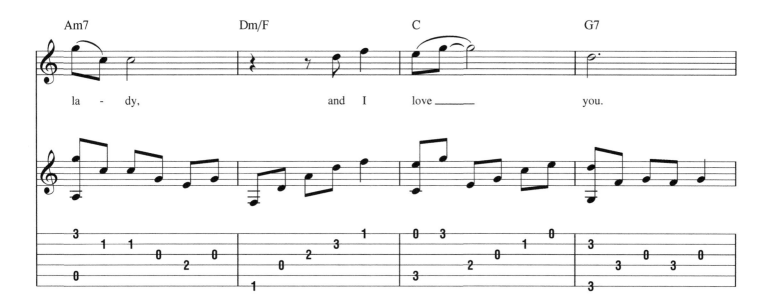

la - dy, and I love _____ you.

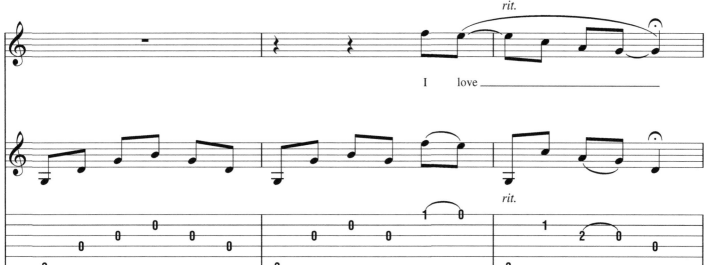

I love _____

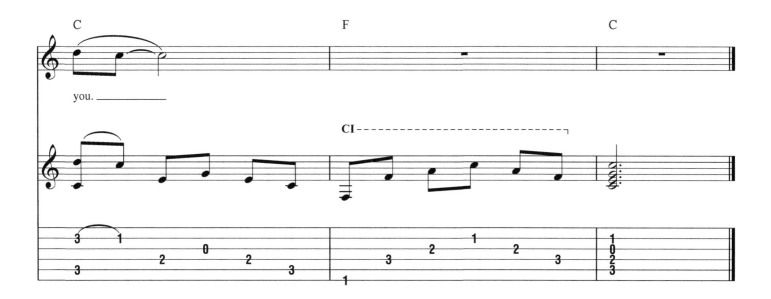

you. _____

Wedding Song
(There Is Love)

Words and Music by Paul Stookey

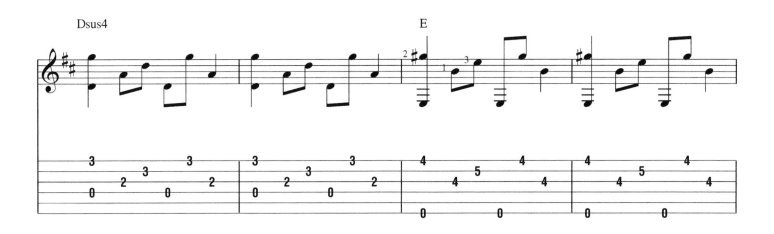

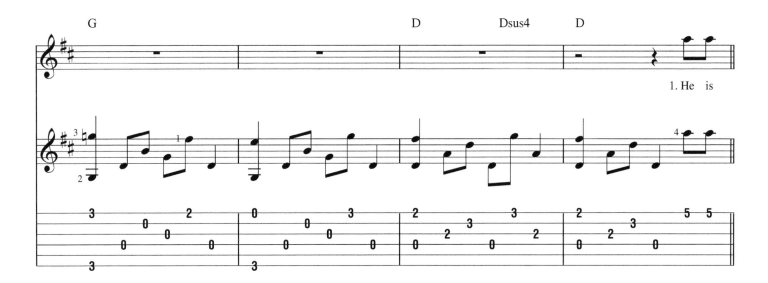

Verse

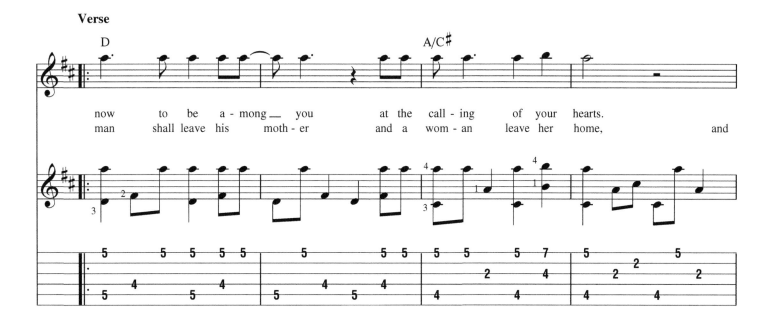

now   to   be   a - mong ___ you   at   the   call - ing   of   your   hearts.
man   shall   leave   his   moth - er   and   a   wom - an   leave   her   home,   and

Rest   as - sured ___   this   trou - ba - dour   is   act - ing   on   His   part.
they   shall   trav - el   on   to   where   the   two   shall   be   as   one.

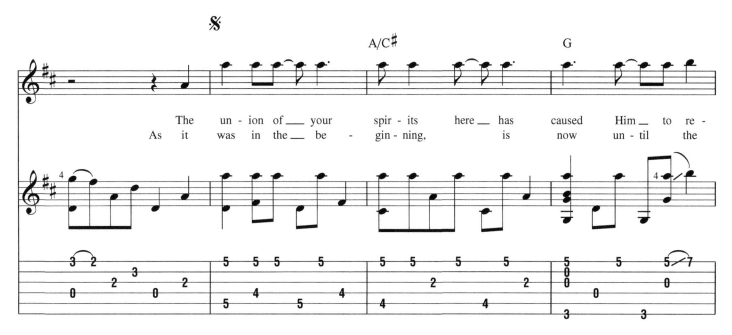

The   un - ion   of ___   your   spir - its   here ___   has   caused   Him ___   to   re -
As   it   was   in   the ___   be - gin - ning,   is   now   un - til   the

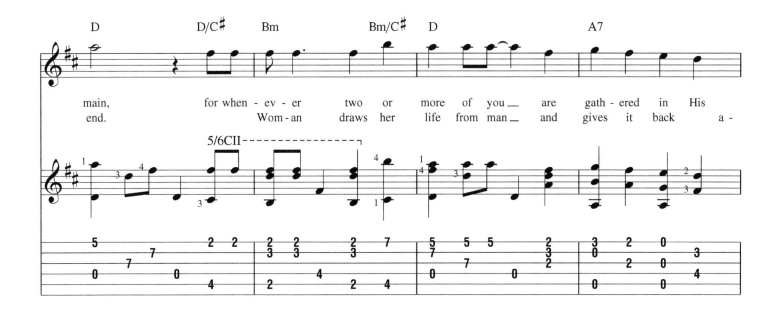

main,   for when - ev - er   two   or   more of you __ are   gath - ered   in His

end.   Wom - an   draws her   life from man __ and   gives it   back   a-

name   there is)

gain   and there is)   love, _____

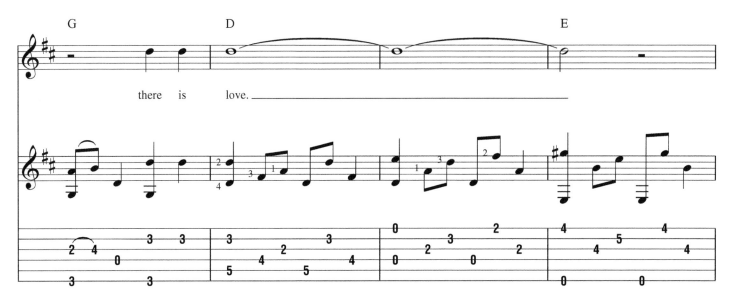

there is   love. _____

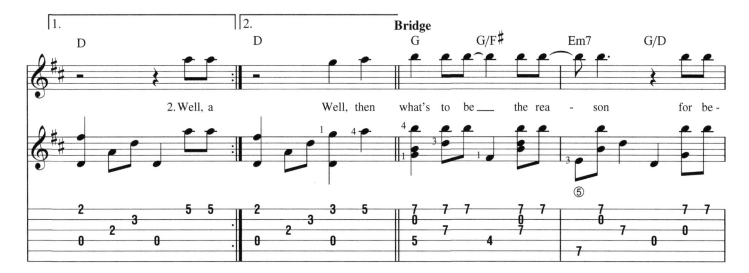
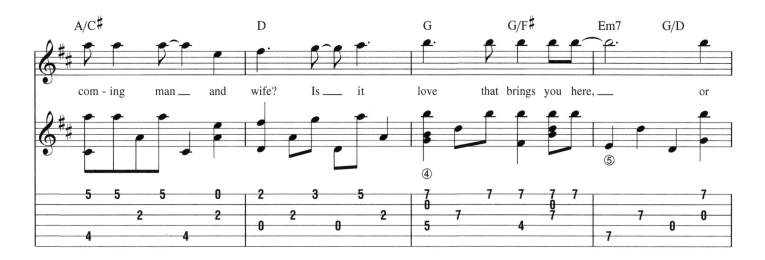
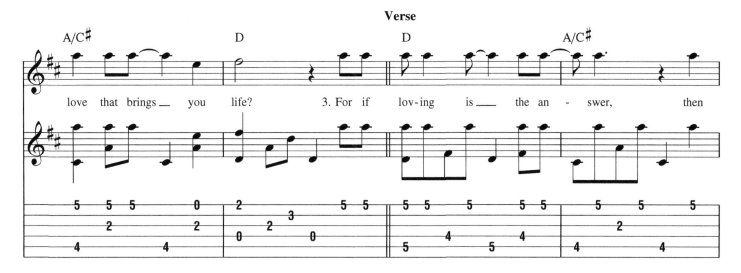

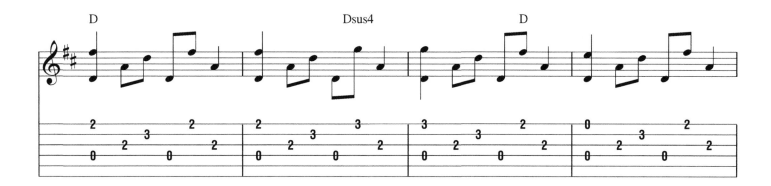

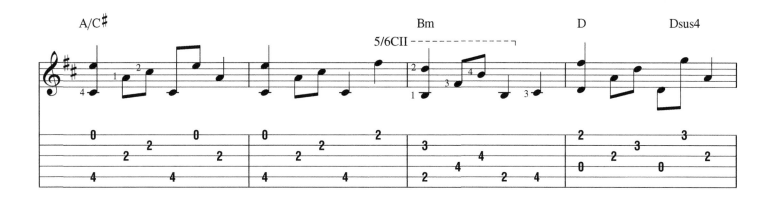

D.S. al Coda
(take 1st lyric)

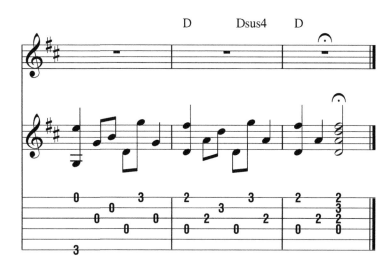 **Coda**

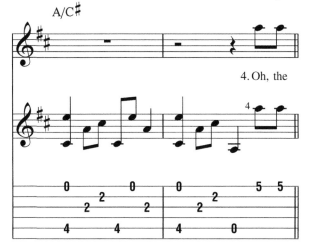

4. Oh, the

What the World Needs Now Is Love

Lyric by Hal David
Music by Burt Bacharach

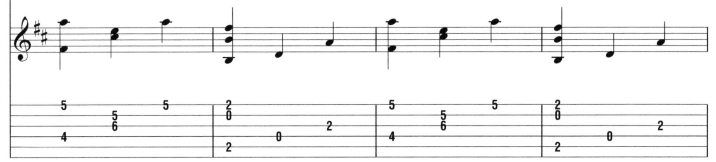

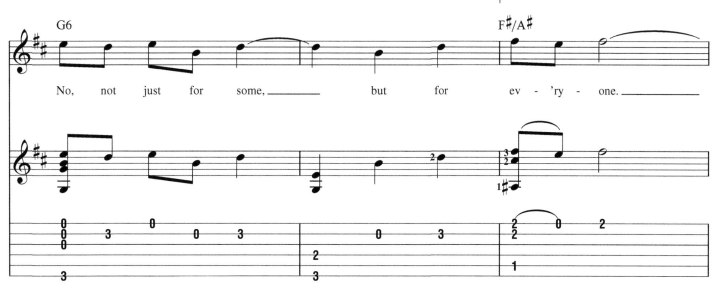

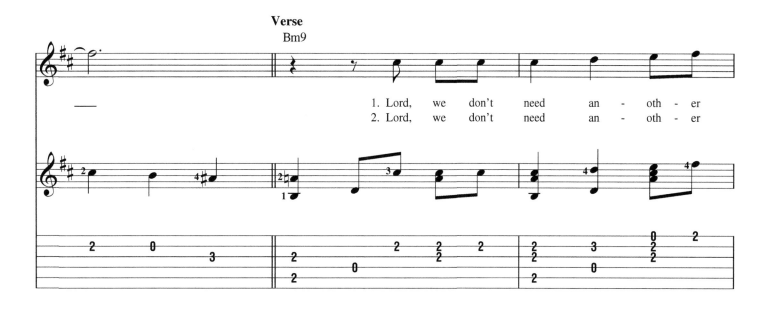

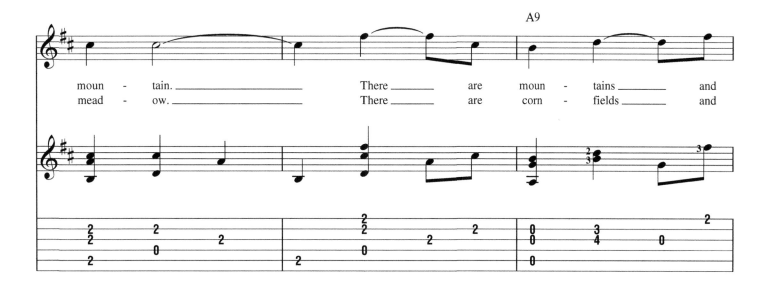

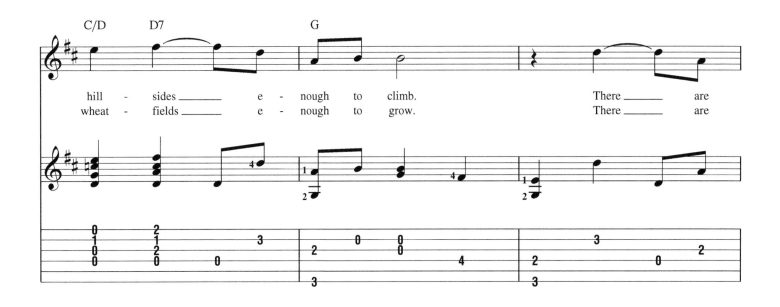

hill - sides _____ e - nough to climb. There _____ are
wheat - fields _____ e - nough to grow. There _____ are

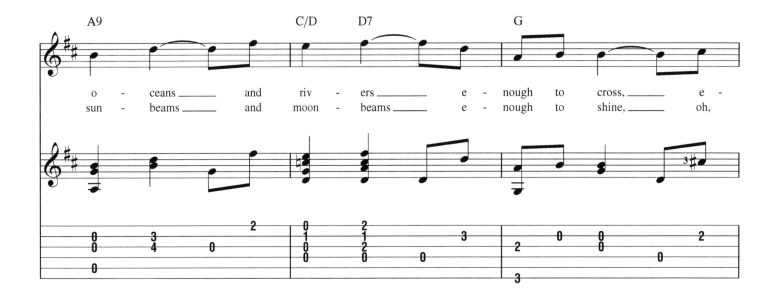

o - ceans _____ and riv - ers _____ e - nough to cross, _____ e -
sun - beams _____ and moon - beams _____ e - nough to shine, _____ oh,

2nd time, D.S. al Coda

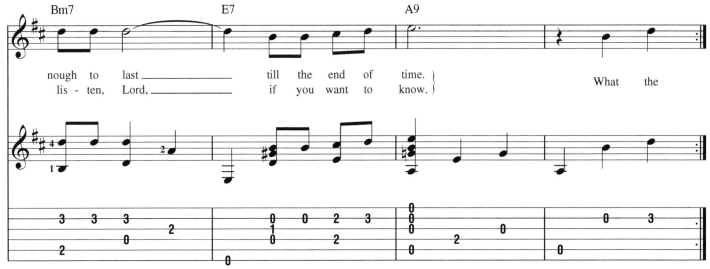

nough to last _____ till the end of time. }
lis - ten, Lord, _____ if you want to know. }   What the

Coda

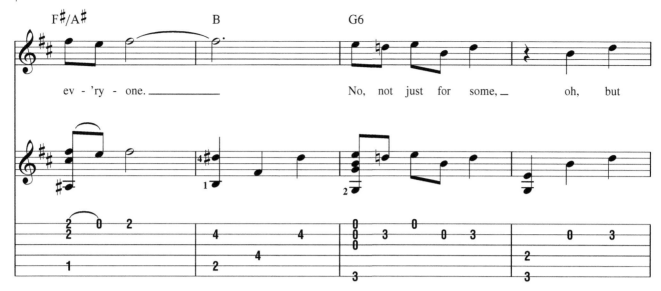

ev - 'ry - one. _____ No, not just for some, ___ oh, but

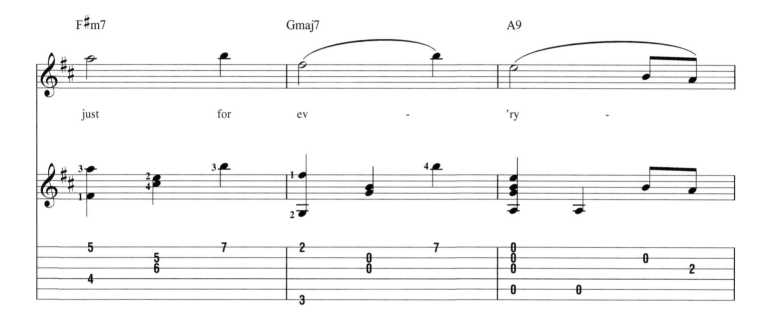

just for ev - 'ry -

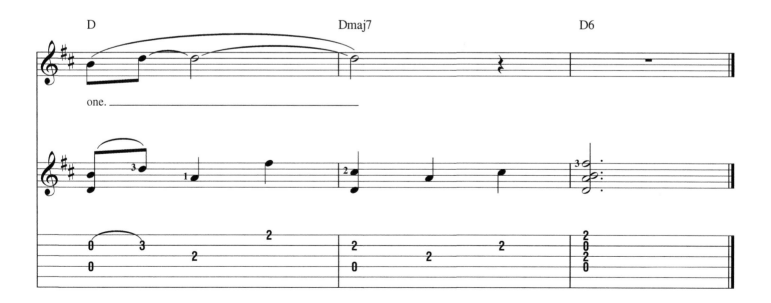

one. _____

You Are the Sunshine of My Life

Words and Music by Stevie Wonder

Drop D tuning:
(low to high) D-A-D-G-B-E

Intro
Moderately

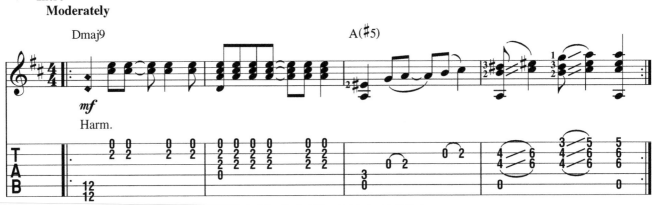

Chorus

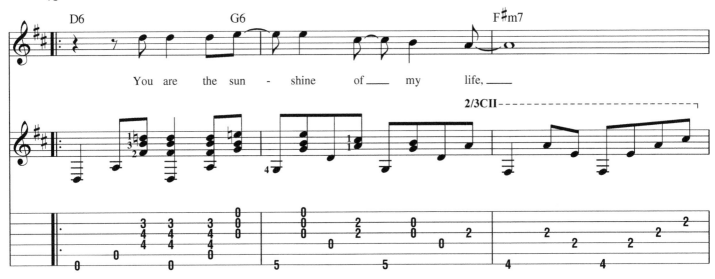

You are the sun - shine of ___ my life, ___

that's why I'll al - ways { 1. be ___ } a -
{ 2., 3. stay ___ }

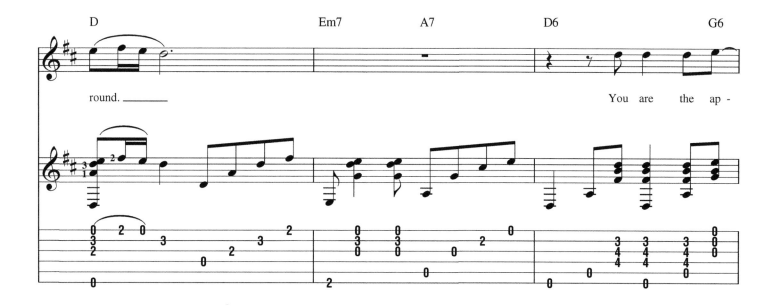

round. _____ You are the ap -

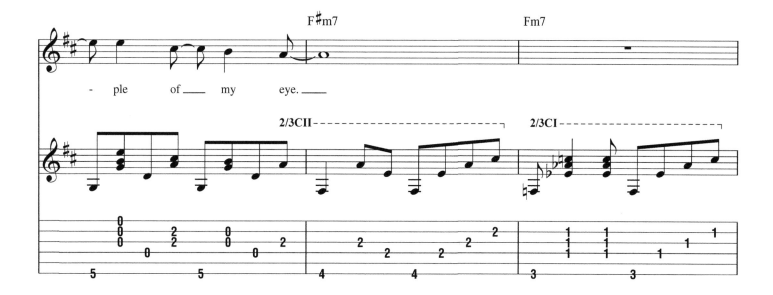

- ple   of ___ my   eye. _____

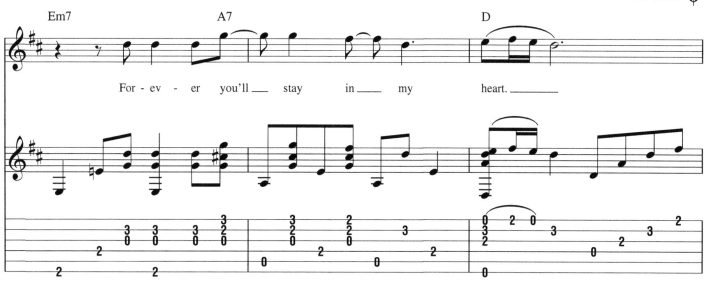

For - ev - er   you'll ___ stay   in ___ my   heart. _____

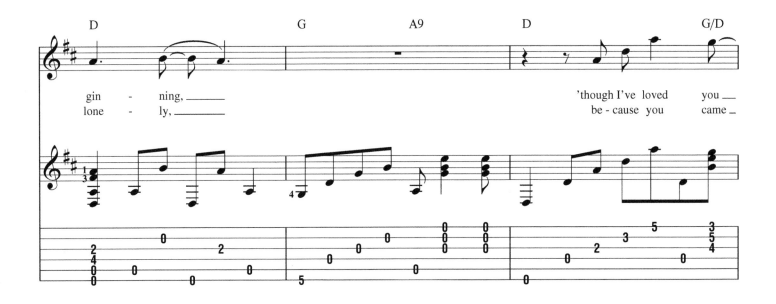

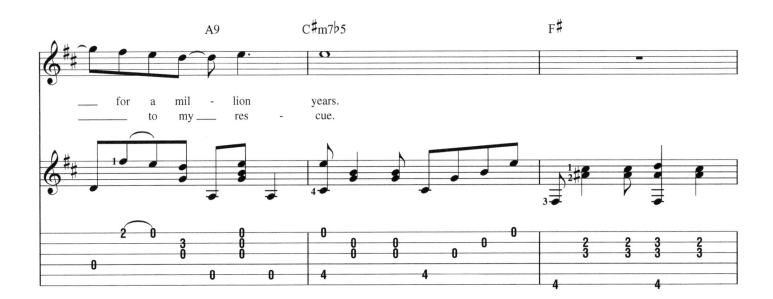

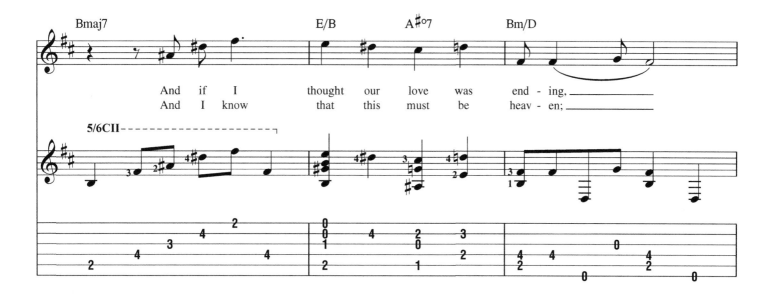

And if I   thought our   love   was   end - ing, _____
And I know   that   this   must   be   heav - en; _____

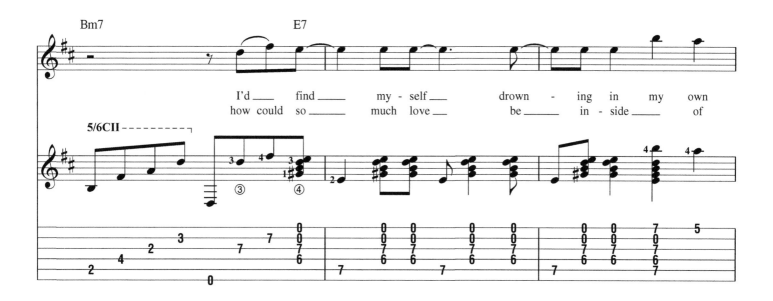

I'd ___ find ___ my - self ___ drown - ing in my own
how could so _____ much love ___ be _____ in - side ___ of

2nd time, D.S. al Coda

tears. _____   Whoa, _____
you? _____   Whoa, _____

Top of the World

Words and Music by John Bettis and Richard Carpenter

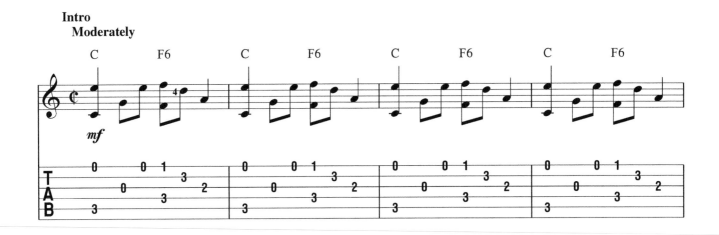

Not a cloud in the sky, got the sun in my
In the leaves on the trees got and the sun touch of the

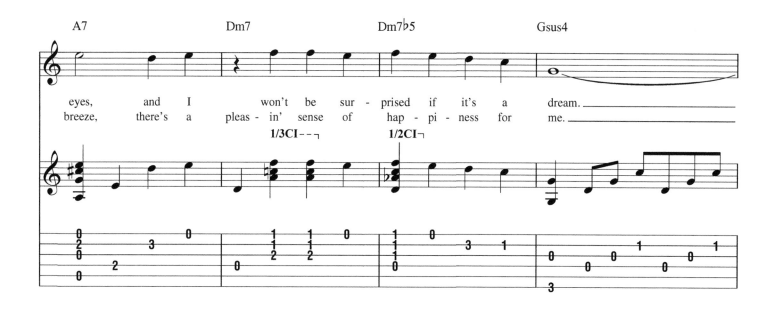

eyes, and I won't be sur - prised if it's a dream.
breeze, there's a pleas - in' sense of hap - pi - ness for me.

Verse

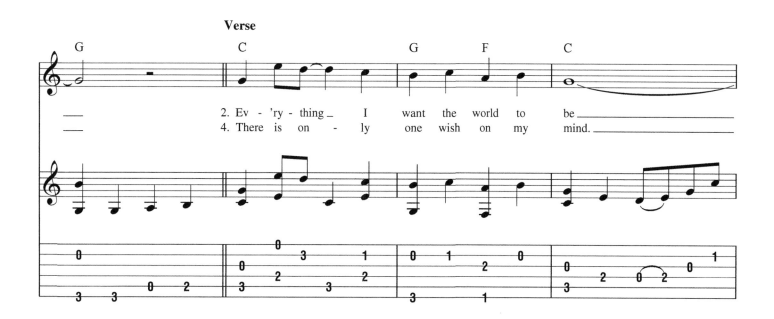

2. Ev - 'ry - thing I want the world to be
4. There is on - ly one wish on my mind.

is now com - ing true,____ es - pe - cial - ly for me.____
When this day is through _ I hope that I will find____

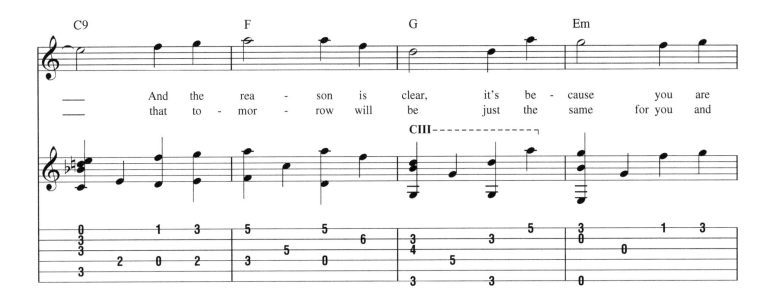

And the rea - son is clear, it's be - cause you are
that to - mor - row will be just the same for you and

here, you're the near - est thing to heav - en that I've seen.
me. All I need will be mine if you are here.

Chorus

I'm on the top of the world, __ look - in' down on cre -

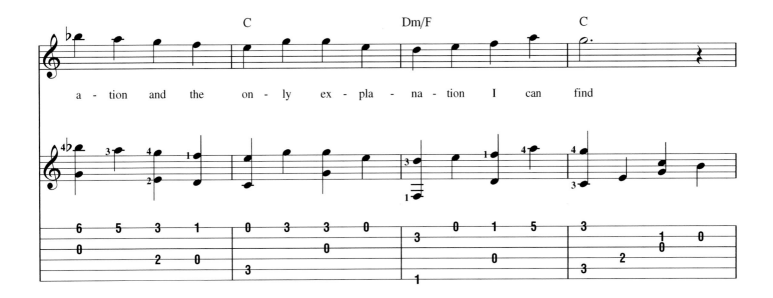

a - tion and the on - ly ex - pla - na - tion I can find

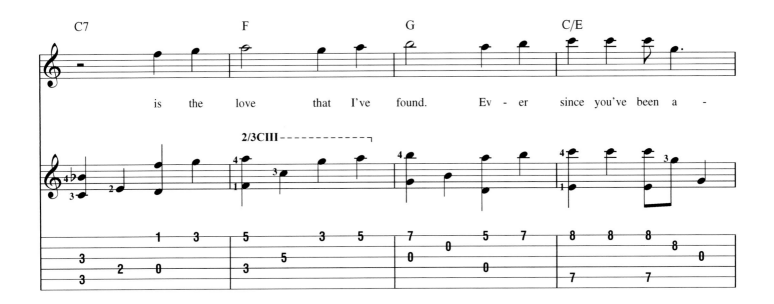

is the love that I've found. Ev - er since you've been a -

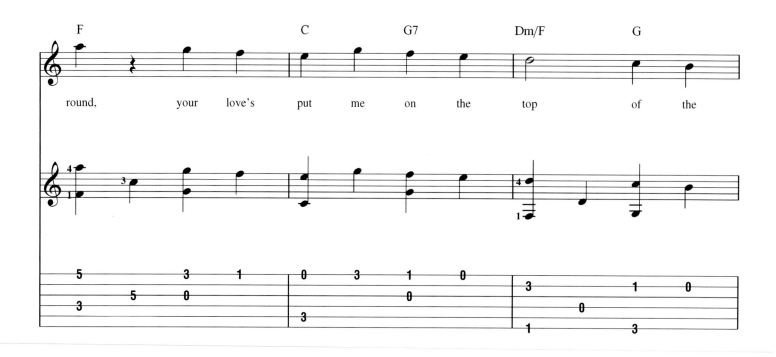

round,   your love's put me on the top   of the

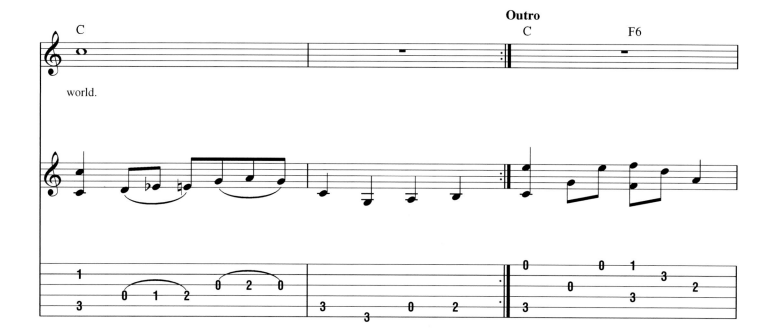

world.

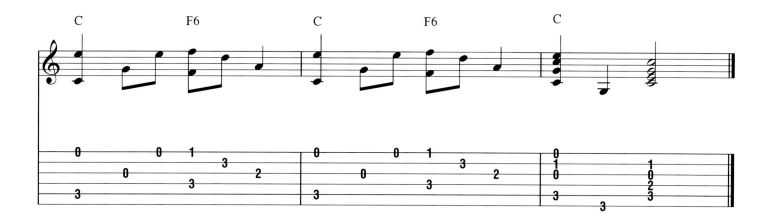